Chandra Shekhar

Bharat Yatra

A BIRD'S EYE VIEW OF A NEW VISION FOR INDIA

CHANDRA SHEKHAR BHARAT YATRA
a bird's eye view of a new vision for india

Sridhara Tumari

Published by:
Prism Books Pvt. Ltd.,
1865, 32nd Cross, 10th Main
BSK II Stage, Bengaluru 560 070, India.
Phone: 080-26714108
E-mail: logistics@prismbooks.com
Website: www.prismbooks.com

Also at:
Chennai : 044-24311266, prismchennai@prismbooks.com
Hyderabad : 040-27612938, prismhyderabad@prismbooks.com
Kochi : 0484-4000945, prismkochi@prismbooks.com

First Print : 2023

ISBN : 9788196152482
Pages : 116 + 4 pages colour inserts

Design : flowergrafic

Book Size : 25.5 cms X 21.5 cms

Printed on : 170 gsm art paper

Printed in India at
Ramya Reprographic Pvt. Ltd.
Bengaluru

Chandra Shekhar

Bharat Yatra

A BIRD'S EYE VIEW OF A NEW VISION FOR INDIA

भारत यात्रा
BHARAT YATRA

श्री चंद्र शेखर का प्रभावशाली व्यक्तित्व आसपास के लोगों को गहराई से प्रभावित करता था।

Shri Chandra Shekhar's dynamism was infectious and visibly enthused the people.

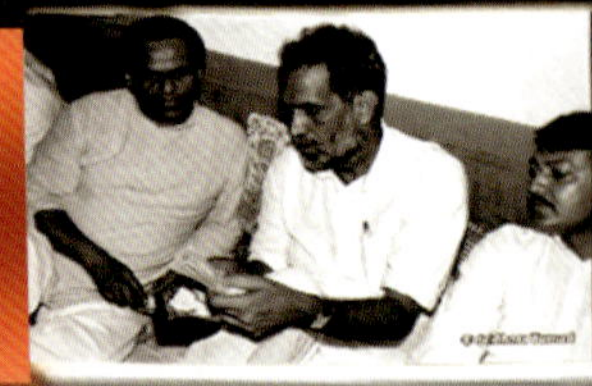

आम लोगों ने अ... दिल्ली तक की ... धनराशि चंदे में ...

People don... spartan lea... padayatra f... Delhi.

विनोद-प्रिय नेता ने अपने चातुर्य-पूर्ण परिहास से अपनी यात्रा के दौरान लोगों के दिल जीत लिए।

The quick-witted leader charmed people all along the route with his sharp humour.

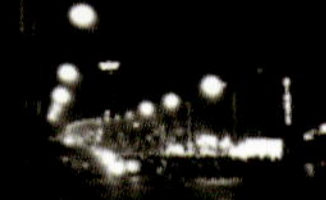

बैंगलुरु के एम.जी. रोड पर पदयात्रा के दौरान शहर की रोशन सड़कों ने कृतसंकल्प नेता का स्वागत किया।

City lights welcomed the determined leader as he walked through M.G. Road in Bangalore.

श्री चंद्र शेखर धै... सुनते हुए।

Shri Chandra... patiently to ...

संध्याकाल में उत्साहपूर्ण यात्रा का दृश्य।

A scene of the enthusiastic march at dusk.

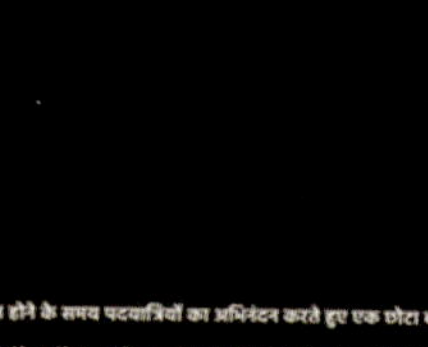

पदयात्रा समाप्त होने के समय पदयात्रियों का अभिनंदन करते हुए एक छोटा बालक।

A child greeting the padayatris at the conclusion of the padayatra.

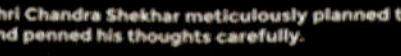

श्री चंद्र शेखर ने विचारपूर्ण ढंग से अपनी यात्रा की योजना बनाई... अपने विचार लिखे।

Shri Chandra Shekhar meticulously planned th... and penned his thoughts carefully.

प्रत्येक गाँव में श्री चंद्र शेखर का परंपरागत ढंग से स्वागत हुआ।

Shri Chandra Shekhar received a traditional welcome in every village.

बैंगलुरु से कर्नाटक सीमा पर स्थित एटीबेले तक पदयात्रा के दौरान श्री चंद्र शेखर अपने अनुयायियों के साथ।

Shri Chandra Shekhar with followers during the iconic padayatra from Bangalore to Attibele on the Karnataka border.

घने जंगल में पदयात्रा को रास्ता बताती वृद्धा। इस अनुभव का श्री चंद्र शेखर की स्मृतियों पर गहरा प्रभाव पड़ा।

An old woman guides the padayatra through a thick forest. The experience left a deep impact on Shri Chandra Shekhar's memory.

यात्रा के दौरान अपने सभी भाषणों में श्री चंद्र शेखर ने उन मुद्दों की ओर राष्ट्र का ध्यान आकर्षित किया जो निर्धन लोगों के जीवन को प्रभावित करते हैं।

Shri Chandra Shekhar raised national consciousness about issues which affected the life of the impoverished in all his speeches during the yatra.

बैंगलुरु के गांधी भवन में श्री चंद्र शेखर अपने विचार प्रकट करते हुए।

Shri Chandra Shekhar exchanging views at Gandhi Bhavan, Bangalore.

पदयात्रा ने दिल्ली से कन्याकुमारी तक पूरे रास्ते में बुनियादी स्तर पर लोगों में ऊर्जा का संचार किया।

The padayatra raised the spirits of people at the grassroots level all along the route from Kanyakumari to Delhi.

कर्नाटक के मुख्यमंत्री राम कृष्ण हेगड़े श्री चंद्र शेखर के भाषण का कन्नड़ भाषा में अनुवाद करते हुए।

Karnataka Chief Minister Ramakrishna Hegde translating a speech of Shri Chandra Shekhar into Kannada.

*Extract from 'Hon'ble Prime Minister **Sri Narendra Modiji's** Mann Ki Baat with Nation April 2022' address regarding Ex- Prime Minister Late Sri Chandra Shekhar's padayatra*

I have come to talk to you all about 'Man ki Baath'. This time, do you know on which subject we received maximum letters and messages? This pertains to our country's past, present and future. I am talking about the inauguration of 'Prime Ministers Museum', on 14th April, this year.

Sri Sarthakji, a resident of Gurgaon visited the museum at the first opportunity and has sent us interesting message through the 'Namo App'. For many years, Sarthakji has been reading newspapers and viewing television news channels; also, he's in social media. Obviously, he thought he's good in general knowledge. But he was surprised after visiting the Prime Minister's Museum because he wasn't aware of many important matters regarding the nation and national leaders. He has talked about many such matters in his letter.

...It seems he came to know about Ex-Prime Minister late Sri Chandra Shekhar's more than 4000 kms of walking to make a historic Bharat Yatra only after visiting the Prime Minister Museum... (The photographs of Sri Chandra Shekhar's Bharat Yatra clicked by well-known photographer Sri Sridhara Tumari is shown)

Due to many such interesting matters, The Prime Ministers Museum is becoming a centre of attraction for the youth and is connecting them to the priceless legacy of the nation. Let their curiosity increase making them read about such matters as well as visit the museum.

We thank the Hon'ble Prime Minister Sri Narendra Modiji and the authorities of Prime Ministers Museum for including this photo series of Sri Chandra Shekharji's Bharat Yatra.

INDEX

FOREWORD

Every object of creation remains unfinished and unfulfilled without the intervention of the divine and spiritual forces of the Universe. I humbly invoke the blessings of these forces and my spiritual master in my endeavor to present this meager offering to my nation, hoping that it will enrich the vision of the leaders and citizens of this great country.

"Vision is the art of seeing what is invisible to the other," quipped Jonathan Swift and aptly so. The vision for the universe and mankind emerged in the mind of the Supreme and hence we as mankind have the Universe, the nature around us and countries to be passionate about, create, and re-design to our own whims and fancies. The world today is immersed in the inventions of the modern era. During the present times, it is beyond one's imagination to think of a padayatra (on-foot march) from Kanyakumari to Delhi's Rajghat covering approximately 4,260 kilometers. This distance was covered by walk by a rare politician, the respectable Chandrashekar, Former Prime Minister of India. It was his endeavor and determination to understand the difficulties and sufferings of personally at their door step. He is the only politician who was able to get a clear picture of the entire country because of the tremendous efforts taken to achieve his goal. This paved the way for him to become the Prime Minister despite a small number of MPs to support him which enabled him to save the country during grave & difficult times.

Roderick Matthews, a writer and Indian historian in his book, "Chandra Shekhar and the Six Months That Saved India," states in his book, "Chandra Shekhar's time in office was short but critical in laying the ground work for the PV Narasimha Rao's Government and the liberalization of the economy that would take place later that year." Chandra Shekhar and the Six Months That Saved India looks at the pivotal role played by the strong man from Ballia, Uttar Pradesh in the transition of power at a decisive juncture and the lesson his tenure holds for India of today. It would not be besides the truth to note that like the proverbial writing on the wall was indeed his Bharath Yatra that played a crucial role and was the force behind his success. The social values like satyagraha, fasting and Padayatra (Dandi March) practiced by Mahatma Gandhi has stayed relevant to this day. However, it goes without saying that there is an explicit need for will power to practice them.

It gives me great pride and privilege to have been the person responsible for documenting the excerpts of Padayatra and hence I have restricted myself to the relevance of the holistic daily routine of Padayatra here. Gandhi initiated the Padayatra of mine workers of South Africa; however, it took a giant step in the form of salt satyagraha or the Dandi March of 1930. An American journalist and a writer, Vincent Sheen describes padayatra as "a symbol of imperishable power over the imaginations of men." The British were stunned by this form of struggle. Nehru regretted for not having visualized its impact, but Gandhi knew about the secret strength and the impact of the Padayatra well in advance!

To bring into context the events that lead to the Padayatra of Chandrashekar is very important without which it will be impossible to justify the means to the end. Chandrashekar was the erstwhile National President of the non-ruling Janata Party in Karnataka, which is the southern part of India. He decided to take this yatra while the elections were in motion. By the time that Chandrashekar completed the padayatra of Kerala, Tamilnadu, and stepped in to Karnataka, the Janata Party won the elections and came into power. It was during this yatra that I had the golden opportunity of moving around with him and it gives me immense pleasure to note that I was able to utilize this opportunity to capture memorable moments at of several events at that point in time. Although it was not possible to photograph everyone who was involved or all the events during such a long journey, I have attempted to present a bird's eye view of his work of a few events exclusively in Karnataka only. I have attempted to organize them together to the best of my knowledge to give the shape of a single day reporting of the Padayatra. This is also a humble attempt to depict the objective of the padayatra by adding social and creative illustration suitable for its basic purpose. I would like to iterate that this is definitely not an album created to record the presence of VIPs or workers who participated in the padayatra as it is humanly impossible to do so. Kindly note that mention of a few names in this narrative does not in any particular manner signify that others have not participated in this great event. I am hoping that all other participants who did not get a mention in this will not mistake this as a deliberate action of omission. This is an honest attempt to provide an opportunity for the future generations to view this epic event with photographs as a historic document!

This book has been arranged and depicted in a consecutive manner starting with the traditional welcome of Chandrashekar, the following announcement, public meeting, long march, breaks & refreshment along with end of the day's sequences in an attempt to record all the happenings of a single day to give the viewers knowledge about the objective and its nature vis-à-vis photographs of a single day's routine. I would like to take the pleasure of noting at this point in time that I was entrusted the responsibility of organizing the printing of the book, "VICHARA YATRIKA," (Travelogue of Reasoning) authored by eminent journalist Sri Khadri Shamanna and also instructed to approach the eminent cartoonist, Sri Ramamurthy for drawing the cover page of the book. Sri Khadri Shamanna was at the point in time the editor of Kannada Prabha, a leading Kannada daily, which was one of the reasons why the book was published on behalf of Janata Party without naming him. It is very important to mention at this point in time the unwavering enthusiasm of Khadri Shamanna who had earlier participated in the "BHOODAAN MOVEMENT" of Acharya Vinobha Bhaave, which was incomparable and way more than any of the youngsters who had gathered and participated in the Bharath Yatra!

Chandrashekar's entry into the land of Karnataka was a historic & epic moment. An entire entourage of like-minded people assembled at Attibele, the border of Karnataka to invite him. Khadri Shamanna and Devegowda were standing on the road in the midst of the crowd to welcome Chandrashekar. The erstwhile Chief Minister, Ramakrishna Hegde was also on the road akin to a common man welcoming Chandrashekar escorting him to the dais with great fervor and respect. One cannot forget how Ramakrishna Hegde translated Chandrashekar's speech to Kannada and ensured that the message reached everyone. Recalling all these memorable events by itself brings upon a lot of joy & pride!

The padayatra of Chandrashekar was very similar to a moving ashram on wheels. His determination to meet poor people of India at their doorsteps was an exceptional message to every politician of the country. Every citizen of the country remembers this historical experience and do believe that it helped him to face the great challenges that arose during his tenure as the Prime Minister of the country.

I want to express my gratitude is to Shri Sudhindra Bhadoriaji who was the planner and initiator of the Bharath Yatra led by Shri Chandra Shekharji, presently Chairman and founder Trustee of the Bharath Yatra Trust in my endeavor to publish this coffee table book.

I shall fondly remember with gratefulness my dear friend, Sri Y.S.V. Datta who has been instrumental in encouraging me to bring out this book. I am grateful to Sudhindra Bhadoria, Chairman and Founder Trustee of the Bharath Yatra Trust, who supported me at every stage and has also provided his article about his experiences as a participant in the Padayatra all through. I am thankful to my dear friend, Ravindranath who has translated some of the Kannada articles to English. I am also thankful to Pradeep Venkatram who has translated extract of Sri Modiji's Mankibath. I am also thankful to Vishwa Sankethi Trust, Mathuru for their generous help. I am thankful to Author & successful Corporate Leader, Ms. Kay. S, who has assisted me with the editing of this book and having given valuable suggestions for the effective presentation of this book. I am also thankful to Sri Shivananda Basavanthappa who has written the sketch for Sudhindra Badhoria's article, to Shailendra Bandagadde who preserved the Vichara Yatrica book and has given it to me to be part of this book. I am further thankful to Sri Harivansh and Sri Ravi Dutt Bajpai the authors of the book, "Chandra Shekhar THE LAST ICON OF IDEOLOGICAL POLITICS" for allowing me to use the Chapter of Bharath Yatra from the book. I am extremely grateful to Frontline for allowing me to use the articles published on the Bharat Yatra.

I thank Mr Pranesh Siravara of Prism Books for undertaking to publish this book and his staff for an efficient production.

- Sridhara Tumari

From Kanyakumari to Delhi For Total Revolution

Bharath Yatra of Chandra Shekhar

Intellectual Travelogue

Ballia district of Uttar Pradesh is extremely beautiful. There is a place called Sitabdeyara where Bihar and Uttar Pradesh meet. That is the birth place of Jayaprakash. Ibrahimpatti of the same district is Chandra Shekhar's town too. That Chandra Shekhar was influenced by Jayaprakash in his childhood years is of no surprise. The “ChaleJao” movement drew lakhs of youth throughout India. Chandra Shekhar was also one among them.

It was natural for the youth of that day to become socialists. The influence of Jayaprakash, the person and his thoughts on Chandra Shekhar was very deep; so too was the powerful influence of Acharya Narendradev. As an ordinary worker of the Samajwadi Party, Chandra Shekhar rose step by step. In between, for a few years, he joined the Congress too. He insisted on progressive programs.; however, it was true that he became disillusioned.

When dictatorship throws itself at you, protest is the only way. After coming out of jail, there was a big revolution in the country. The Congress government collapsed and Chandra Shekhar became the president of the Janata Party. He was a tailor-made leader for this work, a thoughtful, simple person.

The Bharath yatra that had been started from Kanyakumari was not a road measuring task only. It was a well-reasoned tour to sow the values that they believed in into every heart and mind. It is extremely imperative to read its intention. After completing the tour of Kerala & Tamilnadu, they had set foot in the land of Kannadigas. The Kannada land was ready to welcome him. At this point in time, let us delve into a very important question at this point in time in Chandrashekar's own words.

- By Khadri Shamanna

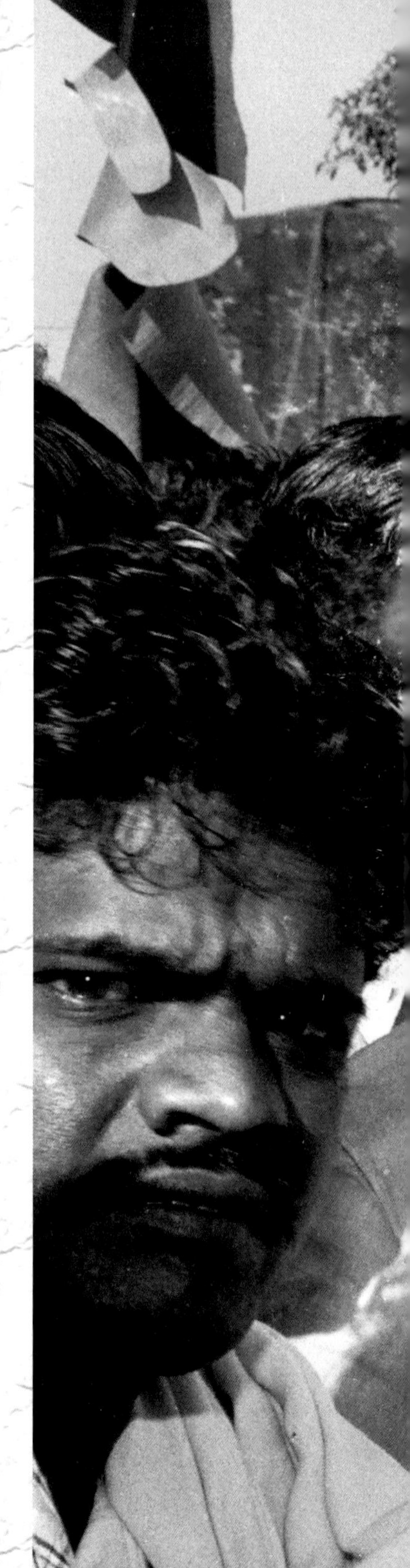

Khadri Shamanna with Deve Gowda at the border of Karnataka waiting to receive Chandra Shekhar's padayatra

CHANDRA SHEKHAR'S INSIGHTS

What is the Bharath yatra for? Several of my friends and critics have asked me the reason for embarking on a Bharath yatra. What purpose will be achieved by this? Will time not be wasted for the tour and thus be disadvantageous to the Janata party of which I am the President? Does it not mean that I am running away from the centre of Indian politics and the Parliament? What is the message that I have to deliver to the common man? What is my alternative plan and the programs through which I have to convince others?

All these are honest questions and rightly so. Why the Bharath yatra as a public servant? It is my duty to give an explanation regarding this. I have answers to a few questions. I don't have answers to a few of my questions. It might be possible for me to answer such questions after completing the India tour. This yatra has not been started as a party program and I did not decide to impose the fire test or ordeal of this tour for self-purification upon myself. Likewise, this tour is not an escape from today's politics; I may like or not like it as a person. The tour was not born out of anger. Also, unlike others, my aim is not to derive instant political benefit from it. From a constructive point of view, the purpose of this Bharath yatra is to meet Indians who have free time but do not have the influence or monetary facilities to inform what they can do about their experiences or how they can resolve their problems. I wish to walk with them, to live with them and listen to them. From this point of view, this Bharath yatra is of an educational nature. Now, the political leadership in India, whether it is in power or not, is trapped in the process of being drawn away from the conditions and the people day by day. Today, the political leaders and public activists are becoming alien to the people whose welfare they should reflect upon and protect. The fissure between them has become so large that the political leaders are behaving as if giving speeches, giving suggestions and making promises is their moral right and only responsibility and that it has become hereditary. Political leaders, irrespective of any party, and many public activists think that they have the ability to solve all the problems of the people and have readymade solutions. But this is not true. If the society has to change fully and the poor have to get the benefits, the process of change has to be based on people's hopes and ambitions and their participation. The true nature of the issues and the understanding of their characteristics and awareness is a preliminary requirement for the social, economic and political change of a society. This awareness should not only be in the people but also in the leaders. In this context, mingling with people, the poor and those who have not received any help from the systematic social tradition is needed.

I have embarked on the tour after the completion of elections in Karnataka and Andhra. This tour was to begin about a month back. I postponed it so that it didn't appear as a part of the election campaign. I decided to start the tour from Kanyakumari before the election results of these states are declared. The purposes of the tour are long-term. Deriving instant benefit is not its intention.

The tour has been started with utmost humility. There is no expectation of any miracle happening from it. If someone thinks that the public will stand up as if a statewide revolution is near because of this yatra; it has to be said that,they are truly in their delusional world. The task of engaging the people is extremely hard. It takes a long time and it probably proceeds slower than the time we are ready to wait mentally and work; still this work has to start. The sooner the first step is placed, the better it is.

The yatra gives an opportunity to get information and to understand the direction and speed of the movement. Why have certain tendencies appeared in the society? Though the country got its political freedom 35 years back, instead of the gap in income and wealth decreasing, why are the poor becoming poorer and the rich becoming richer? Instead of the number of semi-clad Indians and those suffering from hunger decreasing, it has increased from 17 crores to 31 crores. Questions of the population increase being the only reason for the deterioration have to be asked directly and answered. Likewise, the fact stated by official agencies that the number of poor has increased tremendously has to be understood. When the poor are becoming poorer, how are a few industrialist families able to increase their wealth by more than Rs. 100 Crores in a year? If the country's growth rate is slow, why shouldn't the rich share this delay and inefficient national achievement? In the circumstance where the number of hungry is increasing rapidlyand only a few rich are leading a lavish, pompous life of vulgar display, how long can a society, Indian or some other, be able to protect law and order? The income disparity is increasing not just from person to person; this disparity is increasing regionally too. A few regions of a country with extremely rich natural resources are still in the same poor state as they were in the British Raj. Even after getting political independence, why are only towns and cities experiencing wealth prosperity and rural India being neglected despicably? We have to ask these questions.

India is being called a socialist republic. It is being expected that the government shall create policies and programmes that lay the foundation for a society in which an equal economic, social and political position is available to all Indians in the coming years. Leave aside the talk of supplying enough light, basic facilities for sports in schools with medicines and personnel for rural health centres; there are no facilities like school books, slates, pencils for lakhs of children. If the government in the name of "education and youth welfare" spends more than a thousand rupees for the construction of air-conditioned stadiums in the Indian capital, how we can hope that we are proceeding in that direction? If children are not even provided with education and minimum health facilities, leave aside the talk of a casteless society, can we be in the hope that a healthy and happy future will be created for the nation?

Why is the credibility of political parties and political leaders getting damaged so quickly? Why are Indian parties quickening their activities only at the time of voting? Why is political work being considered only as a subject of power politics and politics not being considered as an educational medium and strategy? It should be that this country's people ask the question- Can representatives who spend lakhs of rupees for each election become true drivers to achieve the good of the poor. More than this, people have to cultivate the wisdom that this election system which only gives the opportunity of success to those who can amass enormous financial resources, can never nurture and protect the welfare of the weak and helpless; it is now clear that this system which gives importance to money power and inseminates corruption in public life has to change. How is this change possible? People have to discuss regarding this and create a consensus.

The government and political parties in power are bragging endlessly. Distorted vision and wrong assumptions are the basis for all that. Indian society's true characteristics and tendencies are different and perturbing. There is no agreement between the government's bluster and the majority of people's real experience. The reason for the fall in the credibility and the Indian political system suffering from uncertainty and insecurity can be understood from this.

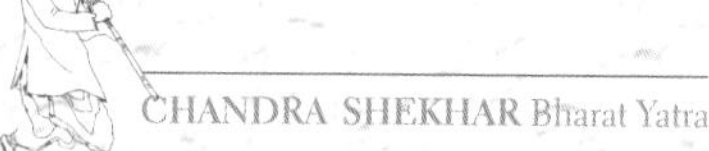

I wish to start this tour not just with regards to the present concern of the nation and the people but also as an opportunity to ask questions deemed important for the future. There only needs to be an exchange of ideas regarding the basis of society and topics regarding its form. I have not assumed that the discussion has to happen regarding any one person or any one party. As time passes, the persons and parties may not exist, but issues and the system will remain. Let us set aside our time for issues and anomalies. Let us identify the basic reasons for the loopholes and distortions in the system. Let us identify the values and ideals from the point of the future and the poor. The driver of the movement and the dissemination of ideas must have the characteristics of the community.

Modern communication tools may perplex the hearts of the people with a simple mind; but they cannot unite them for the goal of purposeful change by infusing inspiration. The entire system is becoming inhuman and is extremely indifferent to the weak and the deprived and has lost the responsiveness for the issues of the minority. This is an indication of the paralysis of fragmentation of the sociability. That is like completely nullifying the struggle of several decades and the heritage obtained from the sacrifice of the national movement too. This yatra will surely be an eye opener and a true life experience.

I appeal to all the people to join in this humble attempt and come forward without considering the strength of the party. My special appeal to this country's youth is that the future depends on how determinedly they involve themselves completely in creating a new era of hope infusing self-confidence in the exploited and the deprived by changing the current social system.

- Chandra Shekhar

Chandra Shekhar Ji's Bharat Yatra
- A New Vision

The 6-month long Padayatra undertaken by our former Prime Minister Chandra Shekhar Ji from Kanyakumari to New Delhi has become an integral part of India's political history. At the commencement of the Padayatra, Shri. S. M. Joshi, a veteran Socialist leader from Maharashtra came to bless the Padayatra. Times have changed since then and with them values and principles of our society along with the Nation have gone through a sea change. Today, the painstaking struggles he and the padayatra is went through during this long and arduous March is unthinkable for most. Sridhara Tumari has meaningfully documented the photographs of this padayatra. His effort has been to cover through photographs and explain in a vivid manner the purpose and meaning of such a unique effort.

Shri Chandra Shekhar Ji, a true socialist understood the value of human connect. He knew that the genuine way of knowing the pains and problems of people was to interact and engage with them at the grass root level. There is no replacement for a physical human effort and contact as well as connect. Therefore, he set out on the padayatra in order to understand his countrymen and their problems in order to try to change the system in favour of the poor, disadvantaged and the marginalized. The issue of water became the core of his concern and focus during the padayatra as we marched across the country. He spoke at the length about implementing the unfulfilled dreams of the Freedom struggle. I had kept close contact with Chandra Shekhar Ji right from my young age and I believed that the padayatra was a very innovative way of connecting with the people. As a part of planning for it, Chandra Shekhar Ji had sent some senior leaders of the Janata Party to study whether the padayatra was a relevant tool to do public work and whether it was feasible or not. All of them advised him to drop his plans of carrying out the padayatra as it was not relevant for people who were in the pursuit of power. However, he was not satisfied with this argument and therefore asked me to revisit the different states and gather the opinion from the people.

As I understood his wishes and also his intention of doing the padayatra, I saw that there was great enthusiasm and people thought that this was a great idea of Chandra Shekhar Ji and welcomed it with a lot of enthusiasm.

BHARAT YATRA
DRINKING WATER
NUTRITION FOOD
PRIMERY EDUCATION
DIGINITY & EDUCATION FOR SC-ST
CUMMUNAL HARMONY

When I met the people of different regions and got to know of their opinions, I prepared a complete report and presented of it to Chandra Shekhar Ji. He was overjoyed and decided in favor of carrying out this great venture which looked more like an adventure in the beginning, as it meant that we would be walking for over 25 km every day. He gave his consent immediately, fixed the date and asked me to go forward in organizing the logistics and managing the entire padayatra efficiently. It was a great responsibility thrust upon me as I was too young and had no such experience in the past.

When we started the padayatra from Kanyakumari, Janata Party had won the elections in Karnataka and was in the process of forming a Government. He did not abandon his padayatra for power and commenced it on the scheduled date, January6, 1983.This was proof of his genuine intention of connecting with people in order to understand them and their problems rather than be in the corridors and the seat of power.

As soon as Chandra Shekhar Ji and the entire padayatris arrived in Karnataka, Shri RamaKrishna Hegde and the entire cabinet along with the leaders of Janata Party as well as other parties welcomed him with flowers and bouquets. Deve Gowda, S.R. Bommai, M. Raghupathi and Abdul Nazir Sab were there to welcome him in different parts of Karnataka. The hand book, "VicharaYatrika" authored by Khadri Shamanna regarding the padayatra reflected the concept of Bharathyatra of Chandrashekar Ji. When the padayatra came to Anekal, the local prominent Congress leader and Taluk Congress President, Shamanna invited Chandra Shekhar Ji to his home to welcome him with warm hospitality. The entire town was decked up with festivities. When the press reporters asked whether Shamanna, being Congress leader, did the right thing, Shamanna replied that Bharath yatra of Chandra Shekhar Ji was for the welfare of the entire nation and not for the benefit of his own party and further said that everyone should support it. At Chitradurga, the most important and veteran freedom fighter, former CM of Karnataka Shri S Nijilingappa welcomed us in his village in Chitradurga District. Bhai Vaidya and Beni Prasad Madhav were among the senior leaders in the entire entourage of the Padayatris, who from time to time guided and helped during the course of the padayatra. Along the way, several people joined him in support and contributed liberally to meet the expenditure of the padayatra. This really added to his enthusiasm and that of the padayatra is during the painstaking tiresome journey. The impact of the padayatra was clearly visible on the governance of Janata Party rule in Karnataka. They took up the issue of drinking water on a priority basis and also implemented the decentralization of power through the revolutionary Panchayat Raj bill. In view of all this, the Bharat yatra of Chandra Shekhar Ji became very popular in Karnataka. Towards the end

when we marched from Humayun's Tomb, Mark Tully of BBC who was a very well-known journalist came and took a long interview of Chandra Shekhar Ji. Finally, when the padayatra reached Gandhi Samadhi, a sea of humanity walked along with him. At the Gandhi Samadhi, a pledge was taken to continue the spirit of Bharat yatra and to work for the principles which were cherished during the freedom struggle. The social action program was to be carried out by the padayatris around the five-point program namely drinking water, nutrition&food, primary education, Dignity and Equality for SC&ST population, and communal harmony. Towards the end of the padayatra, we had become a like a family. Each one of the padayatris departed with a heavy heart and tears in their eyes. Chandra Shekhar Ji did his best to show a new path and a new vision to the coming generation, and now it is for the new Generation to carry this spirit of altruism forward.

To conclude, I am reminded by his words which he repeated many a times during his last days of life that the Bharat yatra was the highest point of his life. He also felt that the experiment of going to the masses to understand reality from 'Bottom Top' is the right approach in social life. It was the Bharat yatra which gave him the true meaning and purpose of life.

Sudhindra Bhadoria
Chairman and Founder Trustee
Bharath Yatra Trust

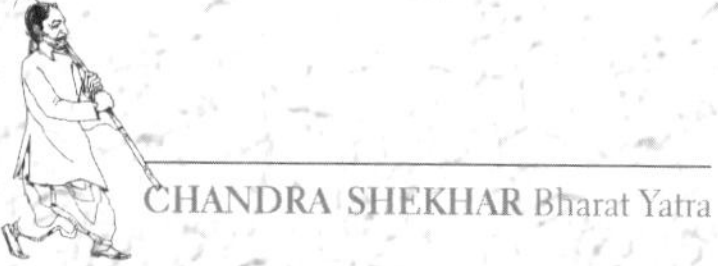

हे राम

CHANRDA SHEKHAR'S PADAYATRA

In September 1981, two young men, N.G. Anthony and V.K. Rajamohan, from the Janata Party, Kerala, came to see him. Earlier, these two young men were members of the 'Radical Forum,' a group that was suspected to be Naxal sympathizers and was banned during the Emergency. Chandra Shekhar was always keen to meet young leaders. Anthony and Raja Mohan met Chandra Shekhar with a proposal to launch a campaign that would lead to the reawakening of the masses. The key suggestion was that among all the opposition leaders, it was only Chandra Shekhar who could meet the challenges of undertaking a padayatra to win back the confidence of the common people in the political system. Anthony and Raja Mohan believed that among all the Indian politicians, Indira Gandhi commanded a pan-Indian presence, and the padayatra would help Chandra Shekhar gain nationwide acceptability to counter Mrs. Gandhi.

Chandra Shekhar sent Dr Sarojini Mahishi and Kishore Lal to access the impact of such a padayatra. They were quite skeptical about the success of the padayatra in creating public awareness and reported to Chandra Shekhar that it would be a harrowing exercise as it might not find popular support among common people. Chandra Shekhar then sent young Sudhindra Bhadoria to talk to the younger generation; Bhadoria's feedback was much more positive. Chandra Shekhar planned to launch his padayatra from Kanyakumari to Rajghat in Delhi towards the end of 1982.Incidentally, just then, the elections for the Karnataka state assembly were announced and the padayatra was delayed until the end of the elections. The Janata Party made significant gains in these elections to emerge as the largest party and eventually formed the government under the Chief Ministership of Rama Krishna Hegde. Chandra Shekhar began his walk from Kanyakumari on 6th January 1983, a day after the Karnataka elections got over. On the very first day, he was joined by around fifty people who accompanied him in this long march.

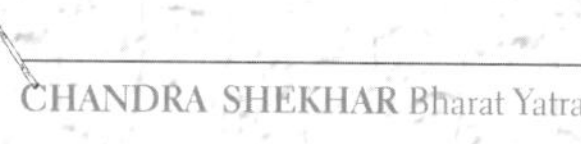

Chandra Shekhar made it clear that the padayatra was not a political programme or a party-based campaignand that no leader or worker was authorized to collect any donations. He declared that every participant would have to depend on the generosity of the local villagers and would have to survive on the food and facilities available. Chandra Shekhar recounted later that throughout the long march, they only had to arrange for their night halt on five occasions mainly because there was no village around. It was the first time since Gandhi's Dandi March that a prominent leader was walking on the foot among the common people to gather first-hand knowledge of their problems and to understand their perspectives. A young man, Suketu Shah, had meticulously planned the itinerary of the padayatra, concluding at Rajghat on 25th June which was the anniversary of the declaration of the Emergency. Chandra Shekhar had planned to walk 25 kilometers every day. A number of his associates were skeptical about sticking to the schedule. They were unsure if each participant could walk at the same pace and were afraid of someone falling ill during the march or some unforeseen situations emerging. Chandra Shekhar took an adventurous approach and said that they should be ready to face any eventuality rather than prepare for every contingency.

On some days, they barely covered 8 kilometers while on other days they managed to walk for 45 kilometers. Chanrashekhar faced a number of health issues during the padayatra and also had some of the most enriching experience. Chandra Shekhar's most unforgettable image was an old women standing outside her hut with a lantern to guide the padayatra while they were passing through a thick forest. At each stop, Chandra Shekhar would address the crowd underline the five most fundamental issues such as drinking water, nutritious food, primary education, dignity for the SC and ST population, and communal harmony. At the end of his yatra in Delhi, some press reporters mocked Chandra Shekhar by saying that after walking for five months and twenty-five days, and travelling distance of 4260 kilometers, all he has highlighted was lack of drinking water. It would be significant to underline that Chandra Shekhar was warning the people of an imminent catastrophe. In contemporary times, the lack of clean drinking water has emerged as the biggest challenge for not just a community, a nation or a continent but to the entire human civilization. That, Chandra Shekhar was a visionary who could look beyond the present and who could connect to the people across the country was firmly established during the padayatra.

Common people donated money to the padayatra at each stop and Chandra Shekhar who started with Rs 3500 at the start of the long march had collected Rs 750,000 by the end of it. He decided to set up the Bharath Yatra Trust (BYT) with this money and spent all these funds on rural development. The first

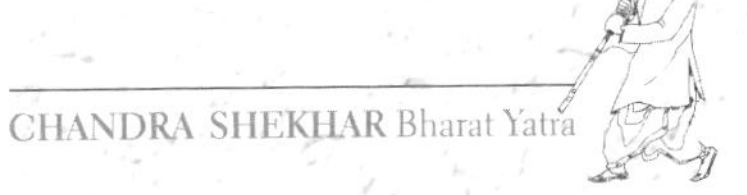

Bharath Yatra Kendra was set up at Arcot in Tamil Nadu and several of these centres were set up in different parts of the country. The management of these centres was handed over to the local people working on similar issues. Ompal Singh, the head of the local village council (gram panchayat) of Bhondsi (Bhubaneshwar) was fascinated with the programmes and wished to donate 100 acres of land for the construction of the centre of the trust. Chandra Shekhar requested only 35 acres and picked a piece of land surrounded by the Aravalli Mountains from three sides. Most of his associates were surprised when he picked such a remote place in a difficult terrain. Chandra Shekhar reasoned that he loved the hills because humankind could build anything but could not create a mountain.

The land was arid, fallow, hilly and full of thorny bushes. To solve the most basic problem of water scarcity, he invited experts, and one of them, Mr. Bali, suggested that the problem could be solved if they could construct a small dam to collect rainwater flowing down the hills. Most people, including Mr. Bali, said that the construction of the dam could be finished in the small window of time before the monsoon. Chandra Shekhar was adamant and the construction was completed before the rain started. The author (Harivansh) himself had visited Bhubneshwari Ashram in 1984; the place looked desolate and barren and there was just one room. Chandra Shekhar sought help from architects, designers artist like Satish Gujral to plan the whole layout of the centre, also referred to as the Ashram. The most inhospitable, infertile and barren land was converted into a lush green area with trees and crop cultivation. During the first eighteen years of the ashram,21 lakh saplings were planted. At a later stage, a training institute and a primary health Centre were also introduced to the campus.

P.S.Prasad gave up his corporate job to work with Chandra Shekhar and became a long-time associate and the secretary and trustee of the BYT. A public interest litigation (PIL) was filed against the allotment of the land to the BYT in Bhondsi village. Prasad remembered that while the hearing on the PIL was going on in the supreme Court, Chandra Shekhar never made any efforts to present his case to the court. When Prasad asked him what would happen should the decision go against the trust holding the land, he replied that he had come to this place (Bhondsi) wearing a dhoti, kurtha and baniyan (vest) and would leave the place wearing the same clothes.

In the 1990s, the newspapers would publish the details of several hundreds of crores that the trust had gathered through the possession of land and property, almost as a daily ritual. It was alleged that Chandra Shekhar and his family had amassed a massive amount of wealth through these trusts, but he never reacted to these allegations and never even made any attempt to present his side of the story. Once P.S. Prasad asked him what would happen to the property and the land after him, Chandra Shekhar said they were not his personal possessions and they would go back to those whom they had come from. Prasad remembered the day when the court decision was announced, seeking the return of ownership to the gram panchayat and the state government. Chandra Shekhar left that very evening with only his clothes and personal papers, never to return.

The Padayatra Carves a Niche in Indian Politics

After Mahatma Gandhi's famous Dandi March, this long walk by a mainstream politician was one of its kind. The euphoria generated during the walk and especially at its conclusion Chandra Shekhar to the center stage of Indian politics. However, this centre stage was not of a party-based, partisan electoral politics. Rather, it was a constructive, party-less, idealogical politics that JP and Vinoba Bhave had pursued. Several of the opposition leaders were worried about Chandra Shekhar's long march. The Congress party itself was nervous and senior Congress leader, Sitaram Kesri told him that the padayatra was the beginning of a politics of fundamental changes. Chandra Shekhar instead chose to stay within the narrow confines of active, partisan and electoral politics and lost much of the lofty moral heights he had achieved after his long walk. Later, he admitted that number of people had advised him to rise above party politics and assume the role of a guiding force like JP. Chandra Shekhar mentioned that while he had no intention of being JP, the thought of giving up party-based politics did occur to him. However, as an active politician at the age of fifty-six, he had not given up on his ambition of achieving personal glory. Upon the completion of the padayatra in 1983, he aspired to leave an enduring legacy of his political and personal achievements either by being in the opposition or one day by serving in the government.

After the long march, Chandra Shekhar had decided to work in 350 backward districts of the country and wished to relinquish the post of the president of the Janata Party. However, he mentioned later, "I could not do this. After the yatra, I became trapped in the politics of opposition; that was my mistake." The moves for opposition unity were afoot by the Chandra Shekhar completed his padayatra; personally, he was not too keen to get involved with these discussions but gave in to the repeated requests from several of his friends. A number of meetings were organized in Delhi, Srinagar, and Pune with leading opposition leaders of that time.

- From "The Last Icon Of Ideological Politics"
by Harivansh & Ravidutt Bajpai

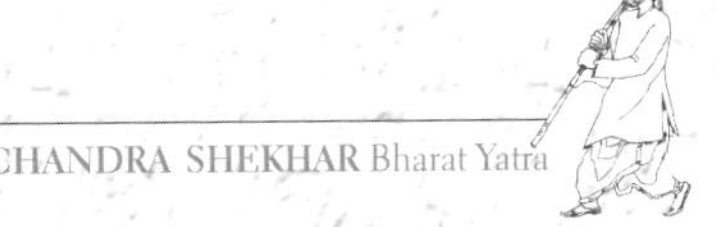

FRONTLINE

INDIA'S NATIONAL MAGAZINE

A rebel's Journey
Venkitesh Ramakrishnan
Print Edition: July 27, 2007

Former Prime Minister Chandra Shekhar was once the face of the alternative liberal democratic political leadership in India.

ONE of the most enduring images of former Prime Minister Chandra Shekhar, who passed away on July 8, relates to the Bharat Yatra that he undertook as an opposition leader in early 1983. The six-month-long "on foot" journey that the then president of the Janata Party made from Kanyakumari to Rajghat in New Delhi, tra-versing approximately 4,260 kilometres, had the stated objectives of "evolving a first-hand understanding of the problems of the people of India and reviving the rapport between the people and the political class". It was an unprecedented and ambitious initiative in terms of the physical effort involved as well as in terms of political intent. It reflected the leader's resolve to push the limits in order to make a political impact.

During his Bharat Yatra, in Kanyakumari in January 1983.
To his right is his Janata Party colleague S.M. Joshi.
- THE HINDU PHOTO LIBRARY

The promise held out by the Bharat Yatra, the hopes it generated in vast sections of the country's population, the way they were nurtured for a fair amount of time, and the ultimate disintegration of the dreams raised by the Yatra symbolise, in many ways, the political career of Chandra Shekhar.

But Chandra Shekhar was equally resolute when it came to opposing the dictatorial streak in Indira Gandhi. He made no secret of his detestation of the culture of sycophancy that had engulfed the Congress during that period. The conflict on this issue between the two leaders grew to formidable proportions and Chandra Shekhar was one of the first political leaders to be put in jail when Indira Gandhi imposed the Emergency in June 1975. Chandra Shekhar was in jail for almost the entire period of the Emergency, which lasted until the announcement of the March 1977 Lok Sabha elections.

In the run-up to the 1977 elections, Chandra Shekhar joined hands with the legendary socialist leader Jayaprakash Narayan to form the Janata Party, which became the fulcrum of all anti-Congress, centrist and right-wing parties. He was also elected president of the Janata Party.

During the Janata Party regime, too, he criticised from time to time the style of functioning of the Morarji Desai-led dispensation and attempted to bring about some course correction. During this period, he stood firm on the issue of dual membership and refused to yield to the pressure tactics of the Jan Sangh group, which was trying to advance the RSS line.

The Bharat Yatra, in organisational terms, was an attempt to enhance the appeal and impact of this upright political personality. There are enough indications to show that Chandra Shekhar was convinced about initiating a new socio-political developmental agenda on the basis of the Yatra's experience. A large number of speeches he made in different parts of the country during the Yatra emphasised this conviction. He had set up 15 Bharat Yatra Kendras to follow up, consolidate and advance this agenda. The thrust of the agenda was on decentralisation of resources and power, and it clearly militated against disproportionate and monopolistic growth.

The ultimate political objective of all this was clear. Chandra Shekhar wanted to lead the nation as Prime Minister. A large number of his associates have pointed out that right from the early days of the 1977 Janata Party government, Chandra Shekhar was convinced that he would be able to "do a better job" as Prime Minister. His statement that he would contest for the leadership of the Janata Parliamentary Party if Morarji Desai were to demit office was a clear indication of this intent. But the grand plans drawn up by the Bharat Yatra failed to bear fruit. The assassination of Indira Gandhi converted the 1984 elections into an out-and-out emotional affair and pushed aside the distinctive socio-political developmental agenda that Chandra Shekhar was trying to advance. The mass emotional quotient and the sympathy factor were so dominant in the elections that Indira Gandhi's son Rajiv Gandhi rode to power with a massive three-fourths majority. The Chandra Shekhar-led Janata Party could win only 10 seats. By the time the next general elections were held five years later, the Rajiv Gandhi-led Congress had squandered this mandate and was reeling under a spate of allegations relating to "corruption in high places". The Congress could win only 197 seats in the Lok Sabha, while the newly formed Janata Dal, in which the section of the Janata Party led by Chandra Shekhar also merged, won 143 seats.

The elections led to the formation of the second non-Congress government, led by the Janata Dal and supported from outside by the BJP and the Left parties. Chandra Shekhar was evidently of the view that he was best suited to lead the government, but Vishwanath Pratap Singh pipped him to the post. It was once again the dominance of the emotional quotient in Indian politics that pushed Chandra Shekhar behind. V.P. Singh was a Minister in Rajiv Gandhi's Cabinet and had resigned from the Ministry and party to lead a highly emotive campaign on the issue of corruption in high places. Chandra Shekhar's honourable political track record, or his confidence about leading the country, was not good enough before V.P. Singh's emotive appeal.

Chandra Shekhar's political practice changed rather dramatically after this failure. The man known for his principled political practice for nearly three decades started succumbing, periodically, to the pursuit of the politics of pragmatism. He adopted a cynical view about the functioning of the V.P. Singh government. When the government fell following the withdrawal of support by the BJP on the Ayodhya Ram Mandir issue, he walked away from the Janata Dal with 64 Lok Sabha members to form the Samajwadi Janata Party (SJP) and joined hands with the Congress. That move helped him realise his ambition of becoming Prime Minister, albeit for seven months starting November 10, 1990.

His brief stint did indeed justify the conviction that he himself and a large number of his associates and friends had on his capacity to lead the country. He had difficult situations, created by terrorism and an economic crisis, to handle: he addressed most of these commendably. According to a large number of bureaucrats and politicians who had worked with him, Chandra Shekhar was a no-nonsense, hands-on Prime Minister who had a firm grip on problems and an enormous potential for governance. He was the first Prime Minister to engage the Punjab militants in a dialogue, paving the way for a process that ultimately helped resolve the issue.

However, the overall track record of his political practice since the early 1990s was an unpredictable mixture of idealism and prag-matism. He had joined hands with the Congress by virtually folding up his opposition to dynastic politics and related afflictions such as sycophancy and authoritarianism. Yet, he refused to succumb to political condescension and resigned when the Congress accused his government of spying on Rajiv Gandhi.

Chandra Shekhar took a principled position on issues such as corruption and communalism and at the same time promoted politi-cians such as the late Surajdeo Singh, who had sobriquets such as "Don of Dhanbad" and "King of the Coal Mafia". Since the early 1990s, the Bharat Yatra Kendras he had set up in the States of Kerala, Tamil Nadu, Karnataka, Maharashtra, Madhya Pradesh, Gujarat, Uttar Pradesh and Haryana started disintegrating. Not only were the centres devoid of any significant activity but the very legal status of many of them came under scrutiny. In 2002, a Supreme Court order held that the Bharat Yatra Kendra in Bhondsi near Delhi had illegally occupied village land.

His party, the SJP, failed to make many inroads into mainstream polity. Chandra Shekhar had to make a number of compromises, even with the BJP, whose Sangh Parivar politics he had openly chastised, in order to retain his traditional seat of Ballia. In the last two Lok Sabha elections, it was the support of the Mulayam Singh Yadav-led Samajwadi Party (S.P.) that helped him return to the Lok Sabha. But, at the same time, he took strong and principled positions in Parliament on a variety of issues that went against the interests of the very same parties. His consistent opposition to the BJP on the Ayodhya issue and his confrontation with the S.P. on the displacement of farmers for the Dadri power project are cases in point.

What this showed was that in spite of the paradoxical streams in his political practice, the socialist from a farmer's family in Ibrahimpatti village in Uttar Pradesh's Ballia district had not lost his basic moorings and perspective. His effectiveness as a Member of Parliament and his steadfast adherence to parliamentary conventions were acknowledged when he was honoured with the inaugural Outstanding Parliamentarian Award in 1995.

There may not be any takers for Chandra Shekhar's political legacy, especially in the context of the virtual non-existence of any political and organisational clout for his party. But his life is indeed a case study that reflects the various positive and negative influences that the country's polity has endured since Independence. In that sense, Chandra Shekhar's life provides valuable lessons to all political practitioners and observers.

Enriching Memoirs From The Padayatra

An unforgettable image for Chandrashekar was of an old women holding a lantern to guide the padayatra as they passed through the thick forest.

Photos **Sridhara Tumari**

Light of the Future

"The sun shines as a sign that I guide you to be a beacon of light for generations to come!!"

Bharathyatra

"Walk Forward & Forge ahead to Victory!" >>>

The Beginning of Padayatra from God's own country, Kerala

Cool camaraderie with coconut water!!

Traditional Welcome

"ATHITHI DEVO BHAVA"

CHANDRA SHEKHAR Bharat Yatra

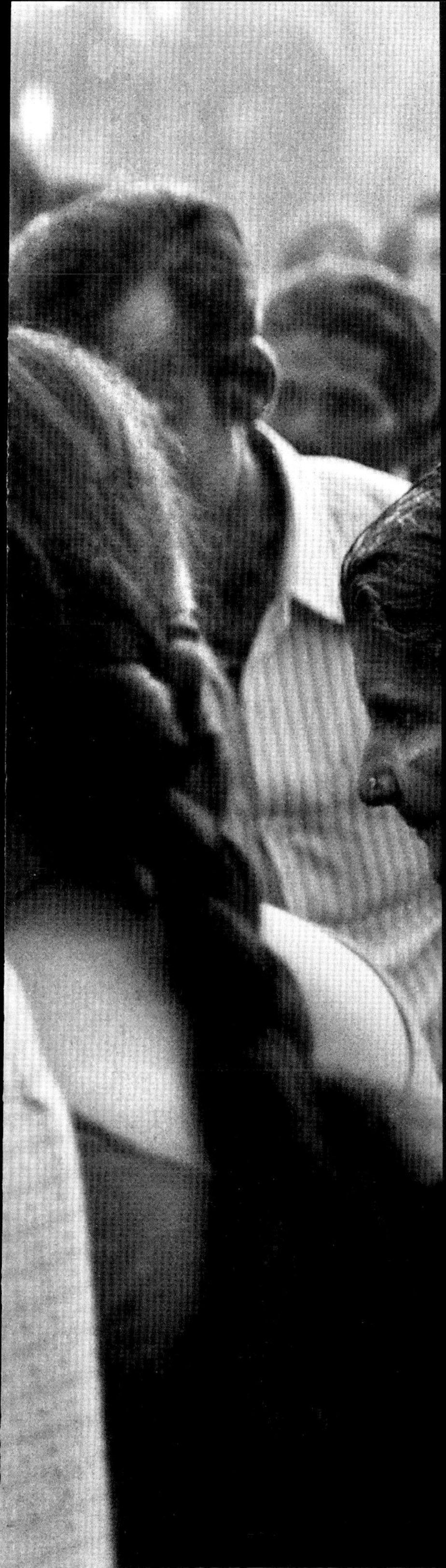

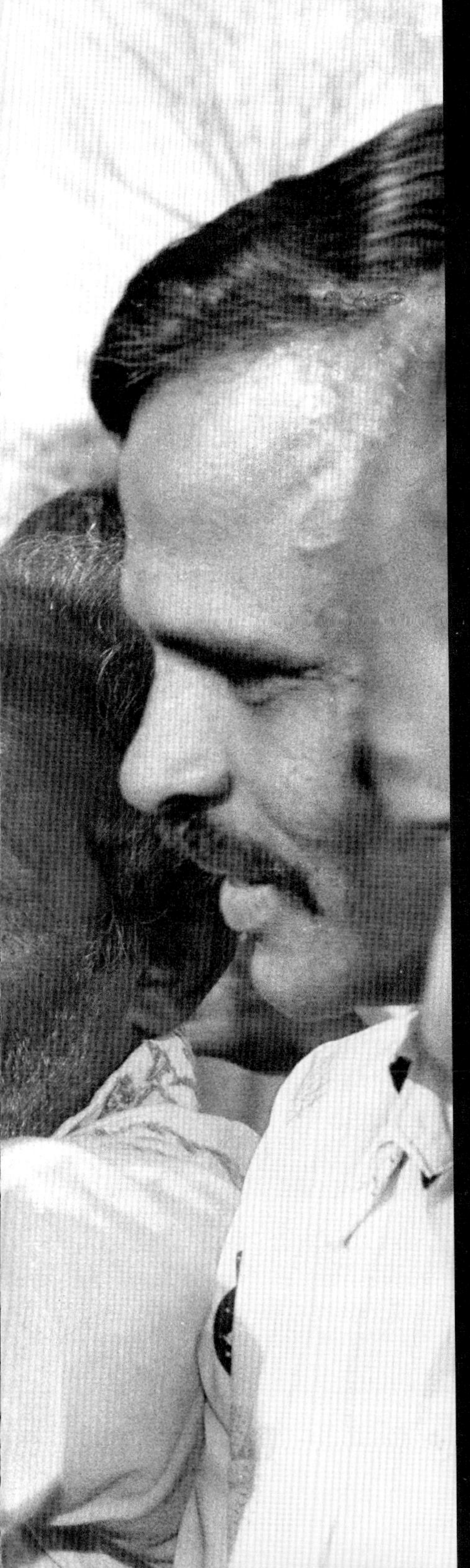

ANNOUNCEMENT

Public Meeting

Yearning for Togetherness

Harmony is my birthright! Community means ME & YOU!

406 SR

CHANDRA SHEKHAR Bharat Yatra

An Intellectual Tête-à-Tête

Bewildered Yet Not Besotted!!!!!!

Will my dreams ever see the light of the day???!!!!

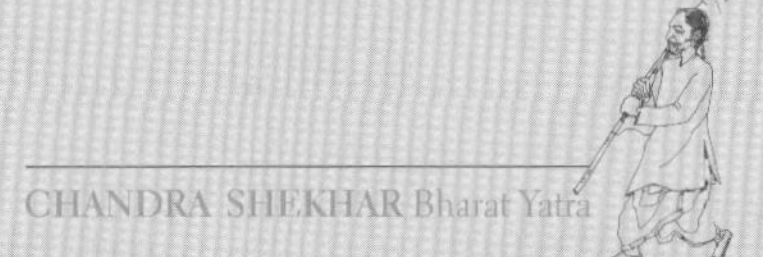

FILM SHOW
ATTENBOROUGH'S
"GANDHI" (English)
(CHARITY SHOW
IN AID OF GANDHI BHAVAN)
AT LIDO Theatre
ON SUNDAY 13th March 1983
AT 2 pm
'GANDHI

LECTURE HALL

A JOURNEY OF A THOUSAND MILES BEGINS WITH A SINGLE STEP

TND
4343

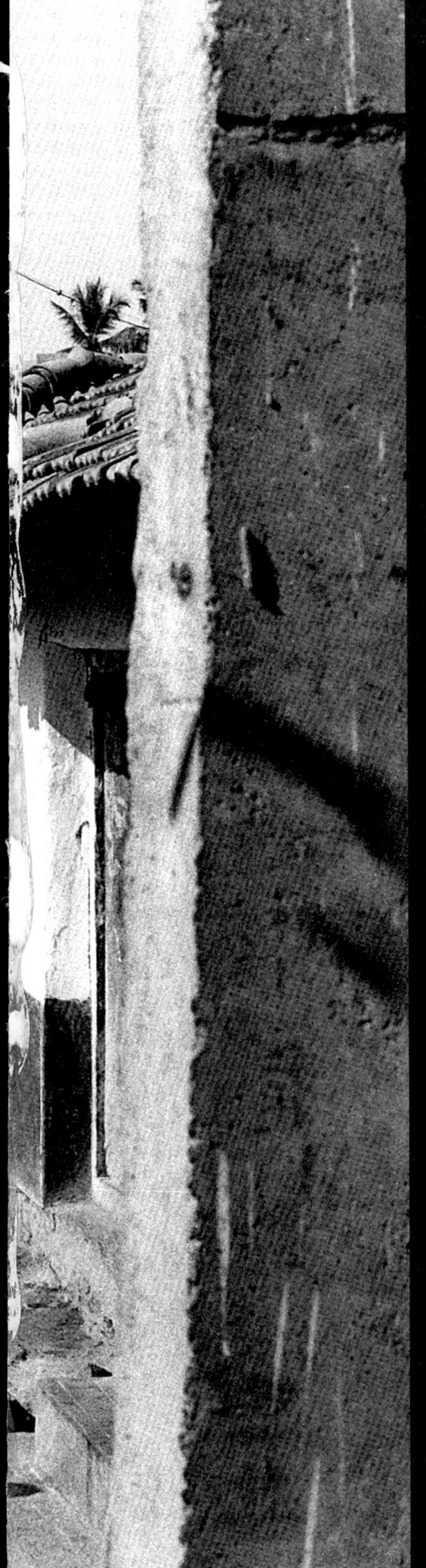

Untouchable ?????!!!!!!!!!!!!!!!!!!!

"The Universe accepts me while you limit me!!"

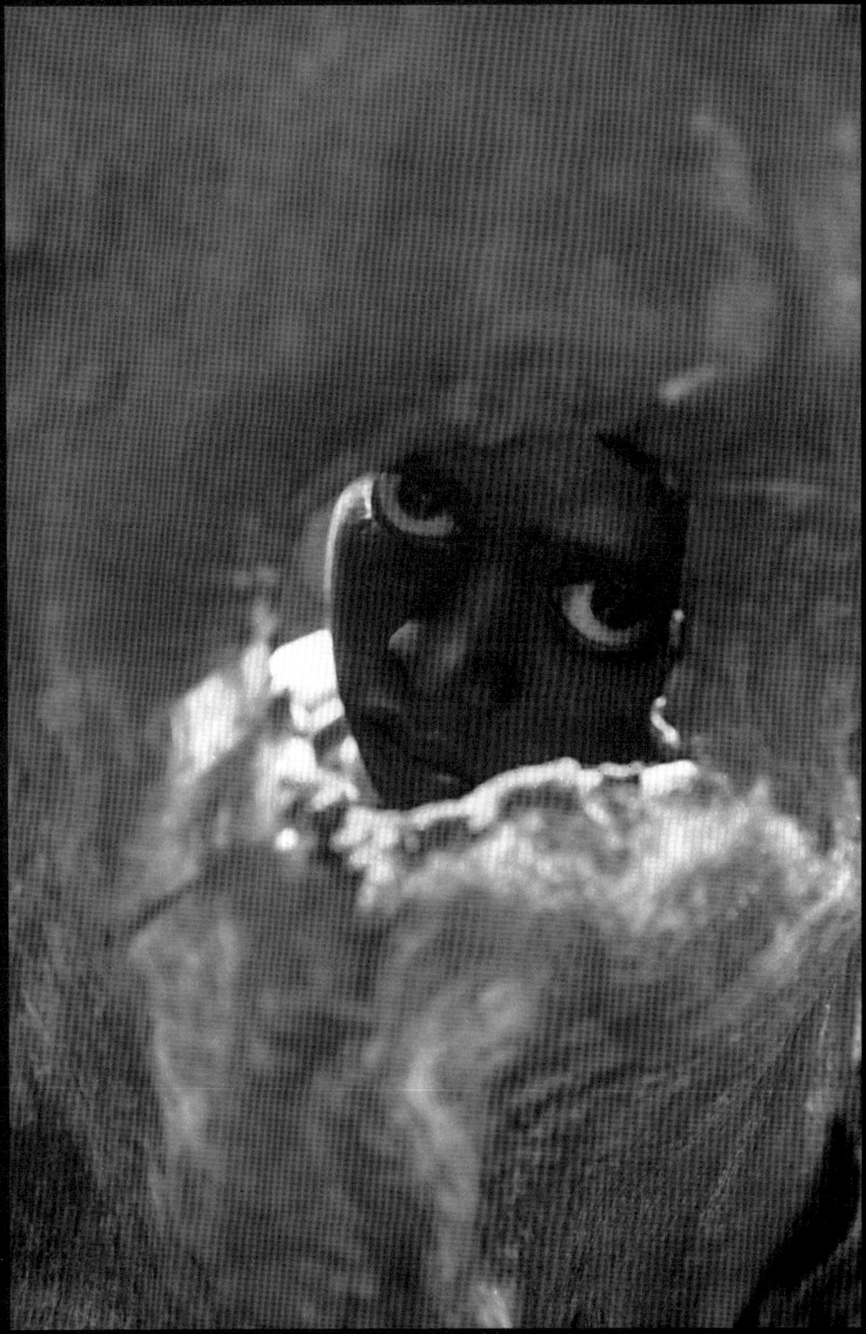

Fear of the Unknown ?????!!!!!!!!!!!!!!!!!

"Your callousness & my innocence do not get along."

Despicable Disparities

You splurge as I suffer!!!!!!!!

Rendezvous on a few steps with **S. Nijilingappa**

Let Your Drama Unfold ....!!!!!

I watch you play your part, but I am aware of mine!!!!!

RIDER

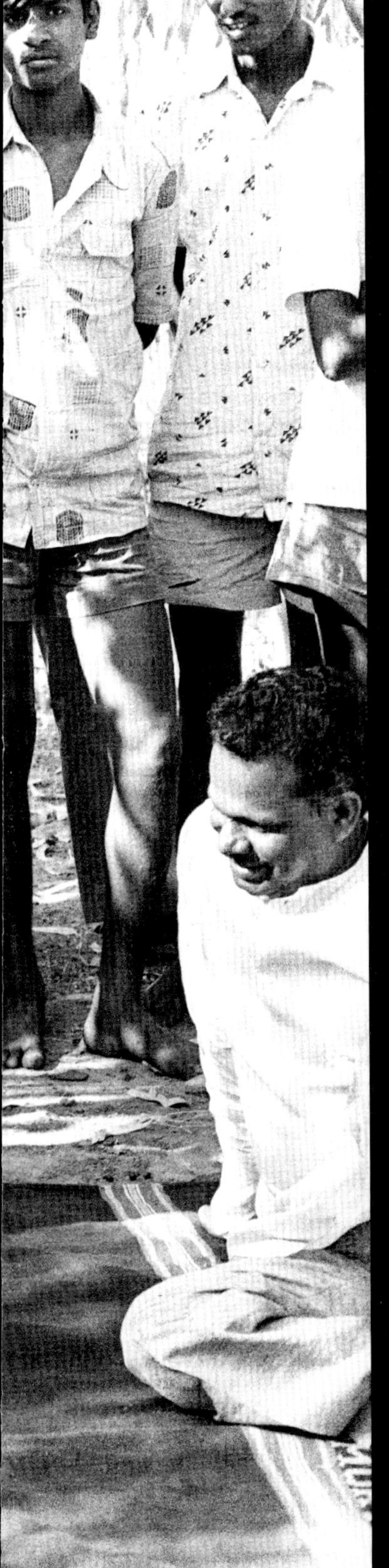

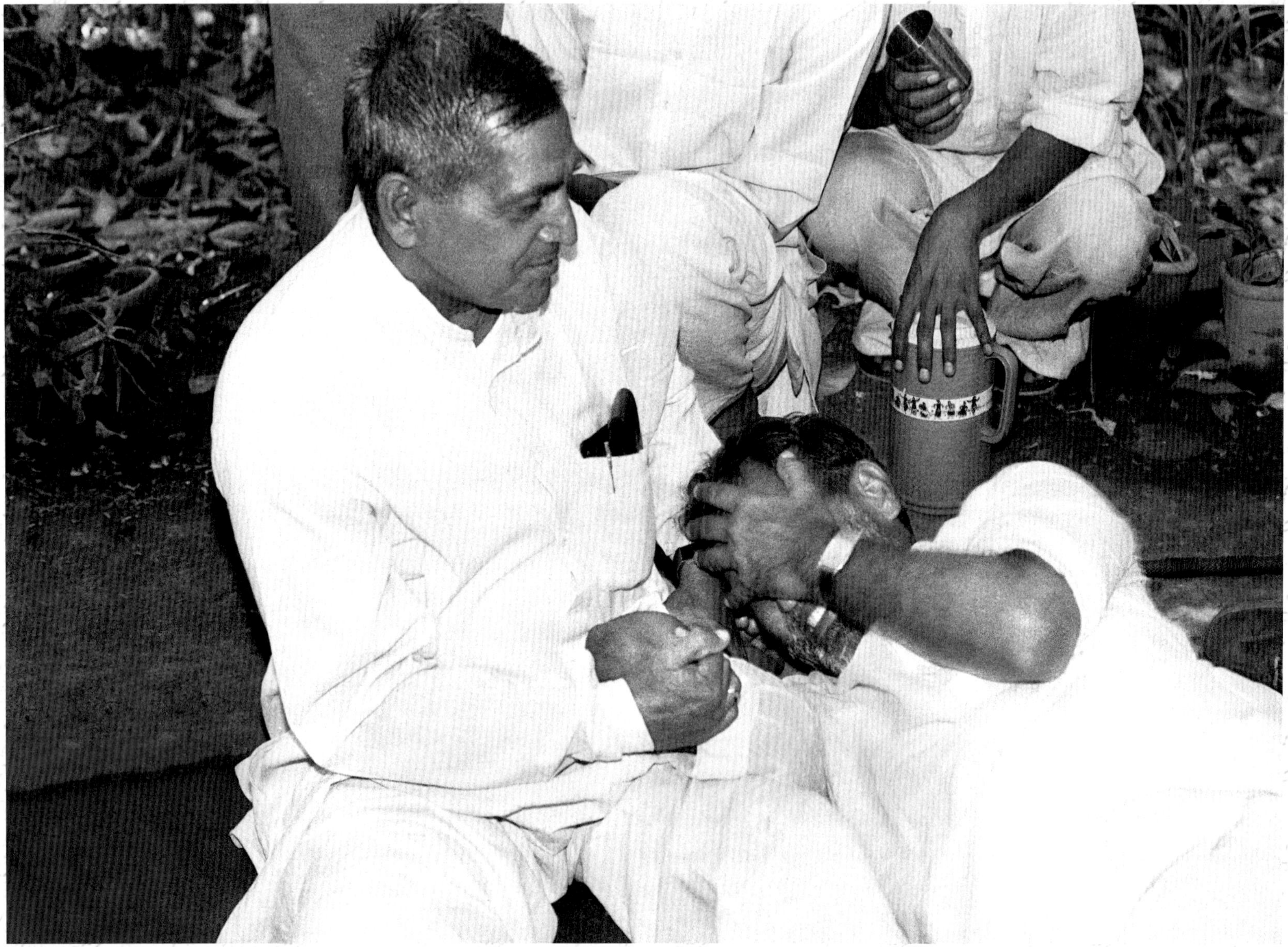

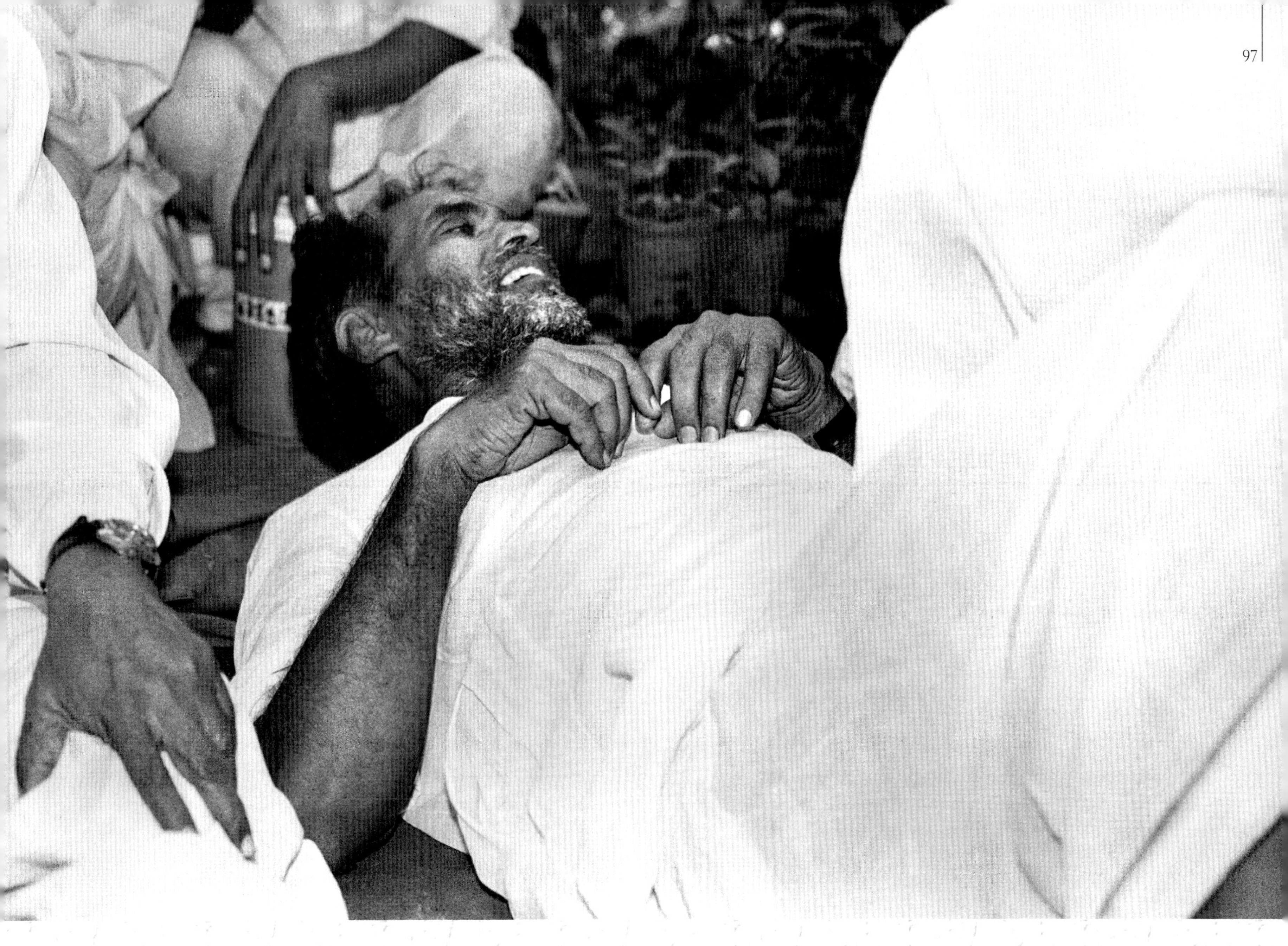

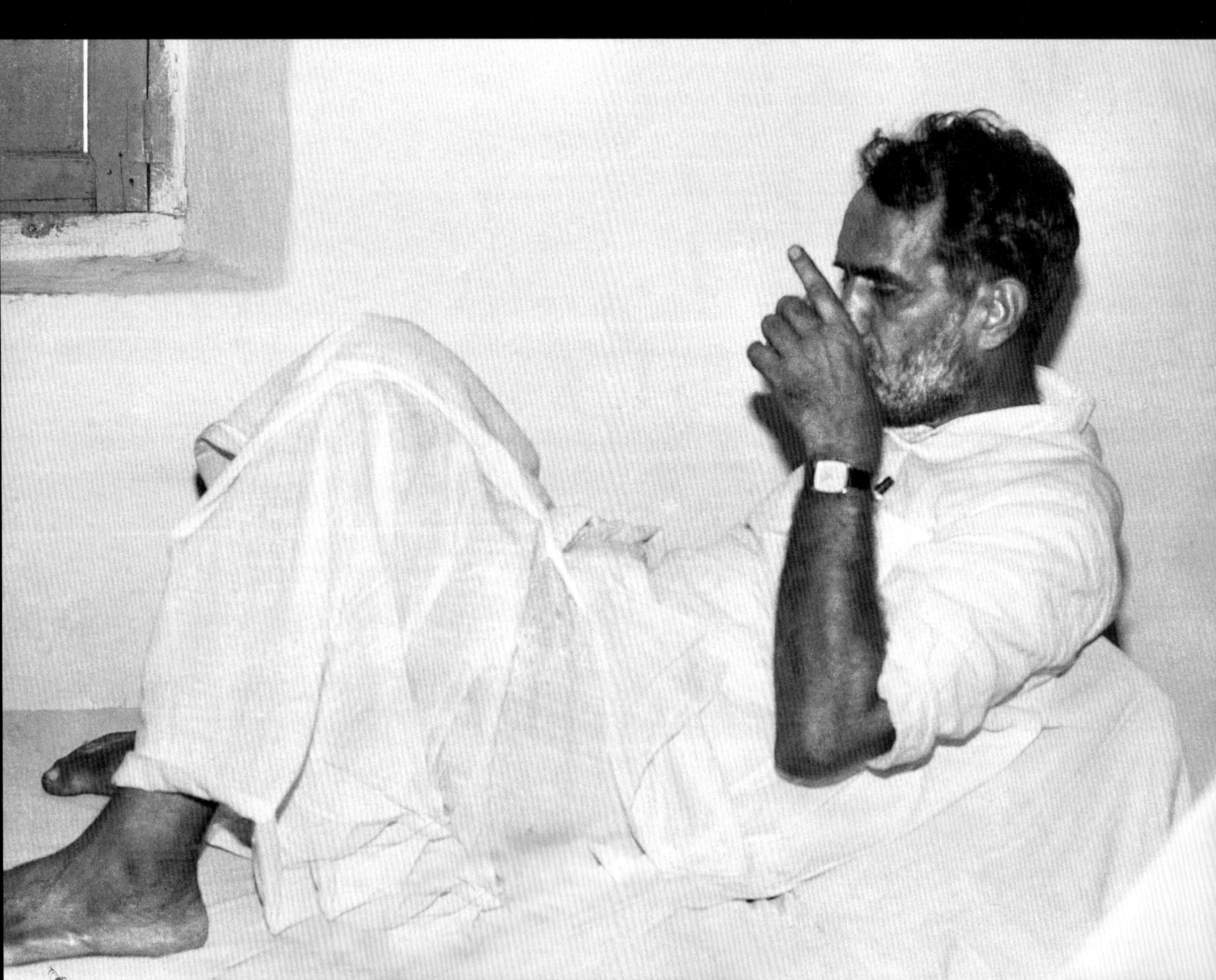

Quenching Your Thirst!!!!!

Water.....Universe's nectar of life!!!!!

And......
We Call It A Day!!

The Wheels of Future wait for None

The clock ticks away as I rue about my tomorrow......

The Bugle of Revolution Beckons !!!!!

Be the change that you would like to see; begin today!!!!

SRIDHARA TUMARI

Freelance photographer and environmental writer. Published several articles in Kannada daily Prajavani, Kannada Prabha along with Sudha and other magazines. Conducted several solo exhibitions of photography in India & Moscow in 1985. Proudly holds the record of having two of my websites namely The World After Nuclear War & Chandra Shekhar Bharath Yatra listed as top trending websites, as Google. I pride also at being one with nature as an agriculturist for the majority of my time.

My motto & aim is to show the mirror of my soul for the world to read, respect & retrospect upon themselves and their actions.

24/11/23

M.T.